explaining...
FOOD ALLERGY

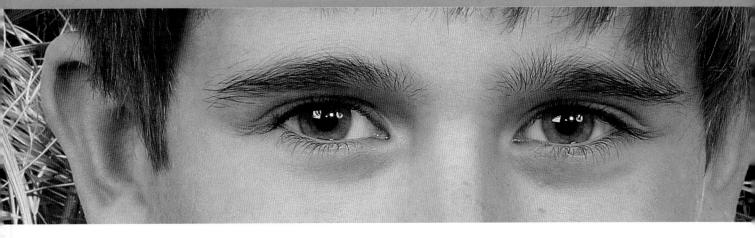

W
FRANKLIN WATTS
LONDON•SYDNEY

This edition 2013
First published in 2008 by
Franklin Watts
338 Euston Road
London NW1 3BH

Franklin Watts Australia
Level 17/207 Kent Street
Sydney NSW 2000

© 2008 Franklin Watts

ISBN 978 1 4451 1773 7

Dewey classification number: 616.97'5

A CIP catalogue record for this publication is available from the British Library.

Planning and production by
Discovery Books Limited
Managing Editor: Laura Durman
Editor: Gianna Williams
Designer: Keith Williams
Picture research: Rachel Tisdale
Consultant: Jane Lucas, Southampton
  University Hospital

Printed in China

Franklin Watts is a division of Hachette Children's Books, an Hachette UK Company.
www.hachette.co.uk

Photo acknowledgements: Corbis: pp. 9 (G. Baden/Zefa), 11 (Betmann), 15 (MedicalRF.com), 22 (Owen Franken), 31 (Dex Image), 32 (Jose L. Pelaez), 33 (Galina Barskaya); Discovery Picture Library: front cover top; Getty Images: p. 36 (Scott Olseon); istockphoto.com: front cover bottom right (Vladislav Mitic), pp. 12 (Carmen Martinez Banus), 13, 16, 18 (Cliff Parnell), 19, 23, 25 (Alexey Kuznetsov), 28 (Jonathan Barnes), 35 (Christine Balderas), 37 (Rich Legg); Photolibrary: p. 24; Ramin Herati: p. 38; Science Photo Library: front cover bottom left (Ian Boddy), pp. 8 (Sheila Terry), 20 (Mark Thomas), 21 (Mark Thomas), 26 (Dr. P. Marazzi), 27 (Paul Rapson), 29 (Sally McCrae Kuyper), 34 (Mark Thomas), 39 (Patrick Dumas/Eurelios)

Source credits: We would like to thank the following for their contribution:
Food Allergy Initiative for Pete and Thomas' story, and www.nhscareers.nhs.uk for Alice's story.

Please note the case studies in this book are either true life stories or based on true life stories.

The pictures in the book feature a mixture of adults and children with and without food allergies. Some of the photographs feature models, and it should not be implied that they have a food allergy.

Contents

What are food allergies?

Do you love chocolate but hate Brussels sprouts? Or love bananas but hate fish?

Many of us may dislike certain foods, but that does not mean we are allergic to them.

Symptoms

A food allergy is not just a simple dislike of a certain food or foods. It is a real reaction by a person's body to the food. This reaction produces symptoms that can range from a mild stomach ache or headache to, in extreme cases, a life-threatening reaction.

The body's reaction

The body's defence mechanisms normally protect us from germs and diseases. But these mechanisms also swing into action when a person with a food allergy eats a food they are allergic to. This should not happen because there is no germ or disease involved. The immune system is responding to something it should ignore.

Different reactions

Some people are allergic to a single, specific food while others are allergic to a wide range of different foods. In some people, an allergic reaction may have mild effects while in others it may have very dangerous effects. An allergic reaction may occur immediately or after a delay of several hours or more. It can affect all of the body or just parts of it.

▶ *Here is a selection of foods which may cause allergic reactions in some people. These include nuts, milk, soya, an egg, bread rolls and bread sticks covered in sesame seeds.*

Doctors can carry out a range of tests to identify which foods a person is allergic to. Once they have this information, the person knows they must be careful to avoid eating the food or foods that will trigger a reaction. In some serious cases, people do not even have to eat the food – just being near it can be enough to make them ill. They may need to carry medicine with them just in case a reaction

begins. Though a food allergy can affect daily life, it is often other people's attitudes that make things difficult for a person with a food allergy.

▼ *Even a children's birthday party can be a dangerous event for someone with a severe food allergy.*

Food allergies: a brief history

Food allergies are not new. Doctors have known about the link between food and illness for thousands of years. However, it is only quite recently that they have understood what happens in an allergic reaction.

Early reports

The first written report of a food allergy was made more than 24 centuries ago by a doctor called Hippocrates, who lived in ancient Greece. He realised that some people had violent reactions when they ate foods that were normally harmless. Hippocrates studied a patient who had a bad reaction to cows' milk, and wrote down all the problems the patient suffered.

Another report was made about 500 years later by Galen, another Greek doctor who lived and worked in Rome for much of his life. He described the case of a child who reacted badly to goats' milk.

Although these early doctors were aware that certain foods could make some people ill, they did not understand how or why this happened. Towards the end of the nineteenth century, answers to these questions began to be found, as doctors began to study their patients' bad reactions to food more closely, recording their experiences in detail. They called these reactions 'food idiosyncrasies'.

20th-century studies

In 1902 two French doctors, Charles Richet and Paul Portier, first used the word 'anaphylaxis' to describe the severe reaction they noticed in some patients. The term 'allergy' was first used in 1906, by an Austrian doctor called Clemens von Pirquet.

During the first half of the twentieth century, doctors continued to observe and record allergic reactions in their patients, but little actual progress was made in understanding the problem. In the 1930s, special diets to help identify food allergies were developed. There were, however, no effective treatments until 1937, when Daniel Bovet, who was working at the Pasteur Institute in France, managed to make a drug that could be used to treat the effects of allergies. This was the first of the antihistamine drugs (see page 26) that are still used today. However, scientists still did not understand why such a drug actually worked.

The discovery of histamine

In 1953, a major breakthrough occurred when Scottish scientists James F Riley and Geoffrey B West discovered that some white blood cells release

▲ *Daniel Bovet and his wife in Paris. His discovery of antihistamine led to the development of new treatments.*

a chemical called histamine (see pages 14-15). At last doctors and scientists realised that white blood cells were responsible for creating an allergic reaction. Another important discovery was made in 1967, when the Japanese husband-and-wife team Kimishige and Teruko Ishizaka showed that other chemicals, called IgE antibodies, were made by white blood cells and were involved in allergic reactions.

Immunology

The field of immunology, which studies the immune system (see page 14), expanded rapidly in the years following the Ishizakas' work. Many more important discoveries were reported one after the other, and scientists slowly fitted together the pieces of the puzzle to explain how the immune system responds during an allergic reaction. Today, research is continuing as scientists try to discover even more detailed information about the process.

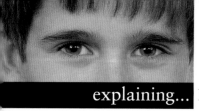

Food aversion, intolerance or allergy?

Doctors estimate that about one or two people in every hundred suffer from a food allergy, although the incidence is higher amongst children. However, many more people than this say they are allergic to particular foods. A recent survey in the UK found that nearly one person in every three thought they had a food allergy.

How can there be such a big difference? The answer is that many people who think that they have a food allergy actually do not – instead, they have a food aversion or a food intolerance.

Food aversions

A person with a food aversion may feel sick just at the thought of eating a particular food. They may find it practically impossible to force themselves to take a mouthful of it, and they will be absolutely certain that it will make them feel very ill. They may even develop physical symptoms such as a skin rash. However, the problem is psychological: the belief that the food will make them ill brings about the physical symptoms. Some dieticians specialise in treating people with food aversions and can help them to overcome them.

Food intolerances

A person with a food intolerance may feel very unwell several hours after eating a particular food. The symptoms often include sickness, diarrhoea and stomach cramps, and their severity depends on the amount of food eaten – the more a person eats

▼ Simply disliking a food means we have an aversion to that food. It does not mean we are allergic to it.

of that food, the worse the symptoms will be. Food intolerances occur when a person's body cannot process a food in the normal way. One of the most common food intolerances is to lactose, a sugar found in animal milks. To digest lactose, the body must produce an enzyme called lactase. If a person does not have enough lactase, they are unable to digest lactose and we say that they are lactose intolerant.

Another food which many people are intolerant to is wheat. People with an intolerance to a particular food are usually advised to avoid eating it if possible.

Food allergies

A food allergy involves the body's defence mechanisms (see pages 14-15). These usually protect the body from dirt, germs and diseases. However, when there is a food allergy, they react to the food as if it is harmful to the body. They spring into action to protect the body from danger – but in fact it is this reaction that can be dangerous, not the food! The reaction usually begins very quickly after the person has touched or eaten the food. The symptoms can be more serious than those of a food intolerance, and involve more body systems. There are various ways in which food allergies can be treated, but most people with an allergy to a particular food need to avoid eating it.

▶ *Some people are allergic or intolerant to some of the ingredients in bread and biscuits. Instead, they may choose an alternative, such as this rice cake.*

PETER AND THOMAS

Two boys talk about their food allergies and how it affects their everyday lives. The first, Peter, is 11 years old. He is allergic to most nuts. He says:

'It is hard being allergic because I can't always do what other children do. For example, sometimes I can't go to my friends' birthday parties, especially if the party is in a restaurant or an ice-cream parlour. Usually, when I am invited to a sleep over, I can't go. I can only sleep over at my best friends' homes because their mothers know what to do for me. I don't know if I'll ever be able to go to stay away at camp like my older brothers.'

Thomas is 11 years old and is also allergic to nuts. He says:

'I have to carry my Epipens (see page 21) with me everywhere I go. Also, I can't eat foods other kids give me like the snacks that they bring to school. Even on Halloween, when I trick or treat, my parents have to check the ingredients of everything I bring home. Usually, I can only keep a few.'

What is an allergic reaction?

An allergic reaction is likely to occur when a person eats a food to which they are allergic. But what exactly is an allergic reaction? What is happening in our bodies when we have an allergic reaction?

Body defence

Our bodies have a complex set of defence mechanisms that protects them from germs and diseases. Together, these mechanisms are called the immune system. Although many parts of the body are involved, the white blood cells play a particularly important role. There are several different types of white blood cell and they each play a different part in an allergic reaction.

First exposure

The first time a person eats a food they are allergic to, they may not notice any symptoms. However, their immune system is being very busy! Chemicals in the food trigger the immune system into action. The chemicals that do this are called allergens. When the allergens enter the body, white blood cells called lymphocytes respond by producing chemicals called IgE antibodies. The IgE antibodies circulate in the bloodstream. As they circulate, they come into contact with another type of white blood cell called mast cells. The IgE antibodies attach themselves to the surface of the mast cells. The mast cells are then primed and ready to 'protect' the body against that food chemical in the future.

1. First time allergen enters body

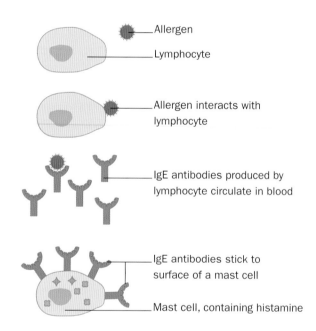

- Allergen
- Lymphocyte
- Allergen interacts with lymphocyte
- IgE antibodies produced by lymphocyte circulate in blood
- IgE antibodies stick to surface of a mast cell
- Mast cell, containing histamine

▲ *This diagram shows how an allergic response develops. There has been no allergic reaction yet, but the system is primed and ready.*

Second exposure

Something different happens when the person eats the food the next time around. This time, the immune system reacts very quickly. The food

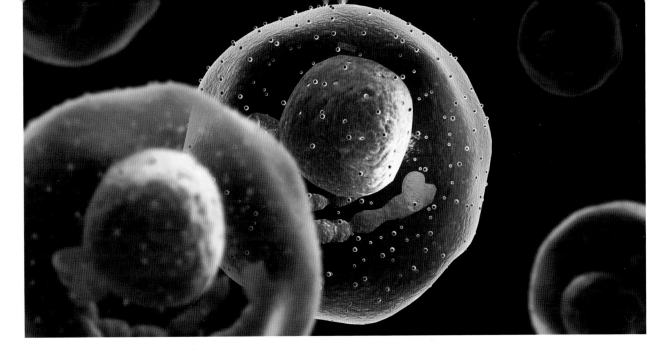

chemical interacts with the IgE antibodies on the mast cells. This interaction makes the mast cells release histamine and other chemicals.

These chemicals circulate in the blood. When they reach the nose, throat, lungs and skin, they can cause a rash and tingling and make it difficult for the person to breathe. They can also cause other symptoms of an allergic reaction, such as sickness and diarrhoea.

2. Next time allergen enters body

Allergen interacts with IgE antibodies

Mast cells release chemicals including histamine. These circulate in the blood and cause symptoms of the allergic response, such as a skin rash.

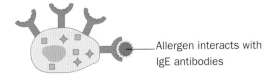

▲ *This diagram shows what happens when the allergen next enters the body and there is an allergic response.*

▲ *These strange-looking objects are mast cells, as seen under a powerful microscope. They contain histamine and other chemicals.*

Specific response

People can be allergic to more than one type of food. Each food contains different allergens. The IgE antibodies must match the allergen exactly. This means that the lymphocyte produces a different type for each food to which the person is allergic.

WHAT ARE IgE ANTIBODIES LIKE?

IgE is short for Immunoglobulin E. There are other immunoglobulins too, called IgA, IgD, IgG and IgM, but although they are part of the immune system they are not, with the possible exception of IgG, thought to be involved in allergic reactions. IgE is Y-shaped. The stem of the Y is always the same. This is the part that attaches to the mast cell. The arms of the Y can be different, though, and it is these arms that match the allergen. For each different allergen, white blood cells can make IgE with arms to match it. It is because of this that an allergic response can be so specific.

Food allergies: common culprits

Different people are allergic to different foods. Some people are allergic to a single food while others are allergic to many foods. It is still unclear why some allergens are so dangerous. Some foods that commonly cause allergic reactions include:

Peanuts

Peanut allergy is one of the most serious food allergies. Even very tiny quantities can trigger a severe reaction. Peanut allergies are often diagnosed in babies and very young children and usually last for life. Although we call peanuts 'nuts', they are not related to tree nuts, such as almonds and walnuts. They are actually related to peas and beans. All the same, people who are allergic to peanuts are often allergic to tree nuts, too.

Tree nuts

There are many kinds of tree nuts, including walnuts, almonds, brazil nuts, macadamias, pecans and cashews. People may be allergic to one, some or all types of tree nut. Tree nut allergies are often diagnosed during childhood and usually last the person's lifetime. Reactions are often severe.

Milk

Allergy to cows' milk is the most common food allergy in babies and young children. Most children grow out of milk allergy by the age of three, but

LUPIN ALLERGY

Lupins are garden plants, grown for their attractive flowers. They are related to peas, lentils and beans. Most lupin seeds contain poisonous chemicals, but sweet lupins do not and are safe to eat. Sweet lupin seeds are increasingly being used in foods such as flour and pasta. Lupin allergy has been known about for some time, and, although it is still rare, it is becoming more common. Lupin allergy can cause severe reactions, including anaphylaxis (see page 20). Some doctors advise people with peanut allergy to avoid lupin seeds, too.

▶ *Lupin flowers like these are found in many gardens. Their seeds are also used in some foods.*

COMMON ALLERGIES

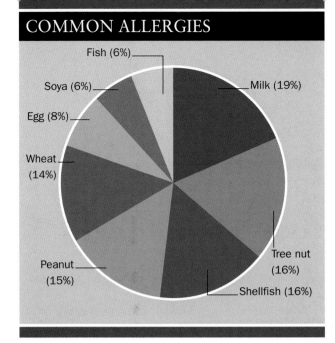

Fish (6%)
Soya (6%)
Egg (8%)
Wheat (14%)
Peanut (15%)
Milk (19%)
Tree nut (16%)
Shellfish (16%)

▲ *This pie chart shows the most common types of allergies in the United States today.*

Milk allergy can affect various parts of the body, causing rashes, diarrhoea, vomiting, stomach cramps and breathing difficulties.

Though peanut allergies are usually severe and milk allergies are typically mild, some people with peanut allergy have mild reactions and some people have died from a milk allergy.

Egg allergy

Most people who are allergic to eggs are actually allergic to egg whites, but some react to the egg yolks as well. Egg allergy usually first appears within a baby's first year of life and by the age of five or six most have outgrown it. Egg allergy may cause mild symptoms such as a rash and eczema, but can also cause stomach cramps, diarrhoea, sickness, a runny nose, sneezing and asthma attacks. Very rarely, an egg allergy can cause a severe reaction.

Soya allergy

Soya is a plant. Tofu is made from soya, and soya is used as an ingredient in many other foods. Soya allergy is a common childhood allergy. Most children

grow out of it by the time they are two years old, but some adults are allergic to soya. Soya allergy causes symptoms that include rashes, diarrhoea, sickness, stomach cramps and breathing difficulties. Soya can cause a severe reaction, though this is very rare.

Wheat allergy

Most people with a wheat allergy react to gluten, a group of proteins found in wheat, rye, barley and oats. Wheat allergy can cause digestive problems, as well as other symptoms, such as rashes, headaches and cramps.

Shellfish allergy

Allergies to shellfish usually develop during adulthood and last throughout the person's lifetime. Many people with a shellfish allergy have a severe reaction if they eat any type of shellfish, but some are allergic to just one type.

Fish allergy

Fish allergies can occur in childhood, but they usually develop during adulthood and last throughout the person's lifetime. Some people are allergic to proteins in a fish's flesh, but some are allergic to the gelatin in fish skin and bones. People may be allergic to just one type of fish or to a range of different fish. Fish allergy can cause severe reactions.

Rice allergy

Rice allergy is most common in countries such as Japan where rice forms an important part of the diet. It can cause breathing difficulties, skin rashes and digestive problems. Rice allergy can cause severe reactions.

Signs and symptoms of food allergies

Food allergies can cause a variety of signs and symptoms. Some are so mild that they are hardly noticed. Others can be severe and make the person feel extremely ill. Some start within seconds, while others take longer to notice. Some involve a single part of the body, while others affect several parts of the body.

If a person eats a food to which they are allergic, they may notice some or all of the following symptoms:

Skin

• mouth, lips, tongue and throat may tingle and swell

• skin in other parts of the body may itch

• a bumpy rash may develop

Digestion

• feeling of sickness

• vomiting

• diarrhoea

Breathing

• difficulty breathing

• asthma attack (if asthmatic)

Circulation

• feeling of faintness

In cases of severe food allergies, the person does not even have to eat the food – simply touching it or breathing in particles of it can trigger these reactions.

▲ *A child starts to feel unwell after having eaten an allergen. Every person with an allergy reacts in a different way when they eat something they are allergic to.*

Differing symptoms

One of the strange things about food allergies is that different people are affected in different ways. This means that two people who are both allergic to the same food can experience a very different type of reaction to it. One person with egg allergy may simply develop a mild rash, while another person may suffer stomach cramps, diarrhoea and sickness.

Another strange thing about food allergies is that a person may react differently to a food on different days. This might depend on how much of the food they ate, what other foods they have eaten recently and whether they are moving around or resting.

▼ *Only 6% of people with food allergies are allergic to fish, but fish allergy can cause severe reactions.*

Anaphylaxis

Most allergic reactions, although unpleasant for the sufferer, are not actually dangerous. One type of allergic reaction is very severe, though, and can be life-threatening. This is the reaction known as anaphylaxis.

What is anaphylaxis?

The sequence of events in an anaphylactic reaction is very similar to that of any other allergic reaction. A person eats some food to which they are allergic and the immune system reacts by releasing histamine and other chemicals. The difference is in the severity of the reaction. Anaphylaxis is often instantaneous and can be very frightening. The throat and airways may swell, making it difficult to breathe normally. The blood pressure may drop, making the person feel faint and weak, and they may collapse and become unconscious. In an extremely severe attack, the person may even die.

Causes of anaphylaxis

Some foods are more likely than others to trigger anaphylactic reactions. Peanuts and tree nuts are the foods most likely to be responsible for

▼ *This doctor is giving her patient instructions about what to do in case she comes into contact with a food that could result in an anaphylactic reaction.*

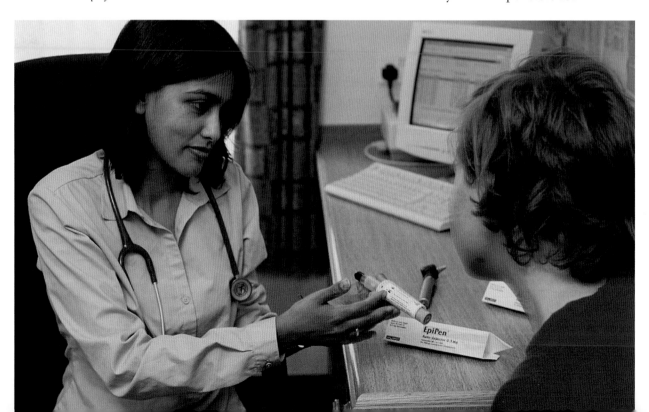

anaphylaxis. Fish and shellfish allergies are less likely to cause anaphylaxis. The reason for this is still not clear.

Treating anaphylaxis

If an anaphylactic reaction begins, the person affected needs treatment immediately. A chemical called epinephrine (also known as adrenaline) is usually injected. To make sure it gets into the body as quickly as possible, the epinephrine is usually injected from an automatic syringe into the thigh muscle. The epinephrine reduces the swelling in the airways so that the person can breathe normally again. It also strengthens the heartbeat, helping to restore normal blood pressure and circulation. Sometimes a second injection is necessary.

Bi-phasic reactions

Anaphylactic reactions can be 'bi-phasic', which means that a person may seem to have recovered, but then suffer a recurrence of the symptoms a few hours later. For this reason, people who have an anaphylactic reaction are usually closely monitored in hospital for several hours until the medical staff are certain the attack is over.

Be prepared

People who know they are at risk of an anaphylactic reaction have to be prepared. They should avoid all contact with the food that they know will trigger an attack. They are usually advised to keep a dose of epinephrine with them at all times. This means that, if a reaction does begin, they can inject the epinephrine immediately.

EPIPENS

An Epipen is a sealed tube that contains a single dose of epinephrine. It can provide vital treatment for a person who is at risk of an anaphylactic reaction, and should be used as soon as the first symptoms of an attack are noticed. The person holds the Epipen in one hand, with the tip pointing down. With the other hand they pull off the safety release. They then jab the tip firmly into their thigh and hold it there for about 10 seconds. During this time, the dose of epinephrine is released into their body. When the full dose has been delivered, a red flag appears in a window and the Epipen can be removed.

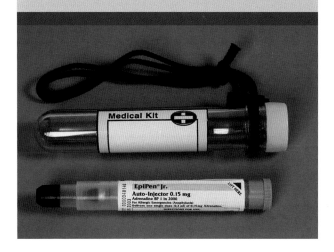

▲ An Epipen like this will deliver a measured dose of epinephrine. It is specially designed so that a person can inject themselves without needing help from anybody else.

Many also wear a medic-alert bracelet, which gives information about their condition and tells people how to help if an attack begins.

Testing for food allergies

How can you tell if you really do have a food allergy? Keeping track of the foods that seem to make you unwell is a good starting point.

There are also several different types of test that doctors and other medical staff can carry out to distinguish between food allergy, food intolerance, food aversion and other conditions that may cause similar symptoms. The tests outlined here should only be done under medical supervision – never try to test yourself as you could make yourself very ill.

Skin tests

A doctor or allergist may scratch or prick a tiny drop of an extract from a food onto the skin, usually on the arm or back. Extracts from different foods can be tested at the same time in rows of separate pricks or scratches. If the skin reacts to an extract by turning red, and often swelling or itching too, the person may be allergic to that food.

▼ *Here, a medical worker is putting tiny amounts of different allergens onto this child's skin. Later, she will check the skin for reactions to find out what the child is allergic to.*

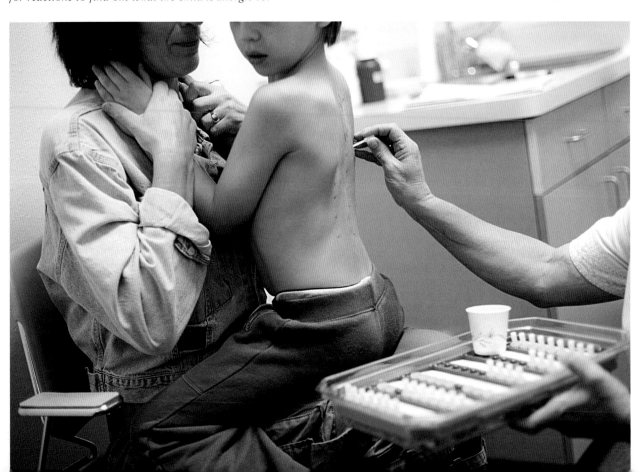

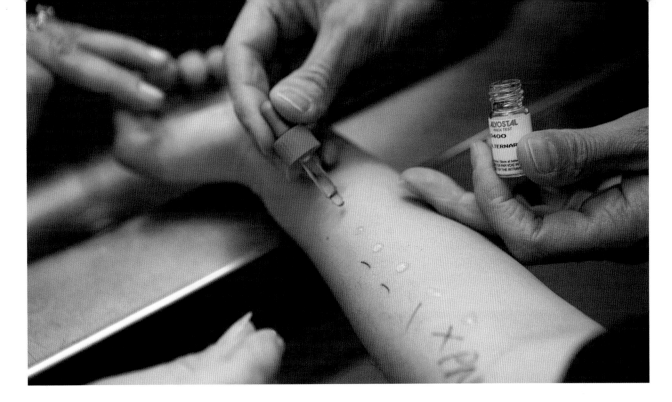

▲ *Drops of liquid, each containing a small amount of a different allergen, are being put onto this person's arm. If a skin rash develops where one of the drops was placed, it may prove that the person is allergic to the allergen it contained.*

If no skin reaction is seen, the person is almost certainly not allergic to that food. Skin tests may not be suitable for people who are at risk of severe reactions, or if they have a skin condition such as eczema. Also, if a person is taking certain medicines, it may make the tests inaccurate.

Food diaries

A food diary is a record of everything that a person eats and drinks, and the times at which the foods are eaten. A record is also kept of any symptoms that the person felt. By comparing the two, a link between a particular food and physical symptoms can often be made, indicating that the person might have an allergy to that food.

Elimination diets

This means restricting the foods you eat to just a few very simple, plain items. Once you are sure that these simple foods do not cause an allergic reaction, you can start adding other foods to your diet, one at a time. Each time a new food is added, you check for any symptoms. If you do not have a reaction, another food is added. This is a very slow, painstaking process, but it can help to identify the foods that are causing allergic reactions.

Blood tests

Doctors may test a small sample of blood to see whether it contains any IgE antibodies (see page 14) that match a particular food. The presence of IgE antibodies in the blood suggests that the person has a food allergy. If none is found specific to that food, the person is unlikely to be allergic to it.

Other tests

A range of other tests for food allergies can be carried out, either at outpatient sessions or during a short hospital stay. Although eye-catching advertisements offering allergy tests often appear in newspapers and magazines, it is usually better to rely on your local medical services – private testing can be very expensive and is not always scientific or accurate.

Avoiding allergic reactions

Most people who know they are allergic to a particular food do their best to avoid eating it. This should be a foolproof way of avoiding an allergic reaction. However, avoiding something is not always as easy as it sounds.

Read the label

In most countries there are strict regulations and laws about the information that must appear on food packaging. The amount of energy, proteins, fats, sugars and salt are usually given, and every ingredient is listed. The label will usually show whether a food contains any common allergens such as nuts, milk and eggs. Labels also carry a warning if a food without allergens has been made in a factory where allergen-containing foods are made, as there is always a possibility of cross-contamination.

Hidden allergens

Often, foods contain unexpected ingredients. For example, some sandwich spreads contain wheat flour, some chocolate bars contain eggs and many ready meals contain soya. This means that, to be sure they are not eating something to which they are allergic, a person with a food allergy has to read every label very carefully indeed.

▶ *A person with a food allergy must always read the list of ingredients in prepared foods very carefully. Supermarkets today have whole sections of special allergen-free foods.*

Allergen-free foods

Many products are now produced especially for people with food allergies. You may see packets with labels such as 'egg-free' or 'wheat-free'. These indicate that they are safe for someone who is allergic to those foods.

Alternative foods

Many alternative foods are also available now. For example, there are some soya snacks that look and taste just like peanuts. Soya milk is a safe alternative for people with allergies to cow or goat's milk. Rice crackers are an alternative to biscuits made with wheat flour.

Not just foods

Food allergens do not just occur in foods. There are some food products that we use for other things too. For example, you might find a shampoo that contains nut oil, or a body lotion that contains wheat germ. A person who is allergic to these foods could suffer an allergic reaction if they were to use such products.

Contact with others

Other people can cause problems for people with food allergies too. For example, if a person eats peanuts, then kisses a person with a peanut allergy, some peanut allergen may be transferred. This can result in an allergic reaction. People with serious allergies need to take care – and make sure their families and friends take care – that allergenic food is not transferred from person to person.

▼ *People with peanut allergy can react to minute amounts of peanut. If this boy has just a trace of peanut on his mouth, he could trigger an allergic reaction in his sister just by kissing her.*

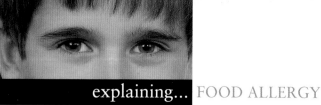

Treating allergic reactions

Because allergic reactions can vary from person to person, there is a range of different treatments available. The treatments cannot cure the allergy but they can relieve the symptoms and help the person to feel better.

Mild reactions

It may not be necessary to treat a very mild allergic reaction, such as one that produces just a faint skin rash or a feeling of mild sickness. After a short while, the symptoms will disappear and the person will feel perfectly well.

▼ *The rash on this baby's arm is caused by a food allergy. The baby may also have other symptoms, such as diarrhoea.*

Stronger reactions

Some stronger, but not severe, reactions can be treated with medicines called antihistamines. These can be useful if the allergy causes unpleasant symptoms, such as a lumpy rash or stomach cramps. Antihistamines work by fighting the effects of the histamine that is released by the mast cells. If a person's symptoms include breathing difficulties, they may be given a type

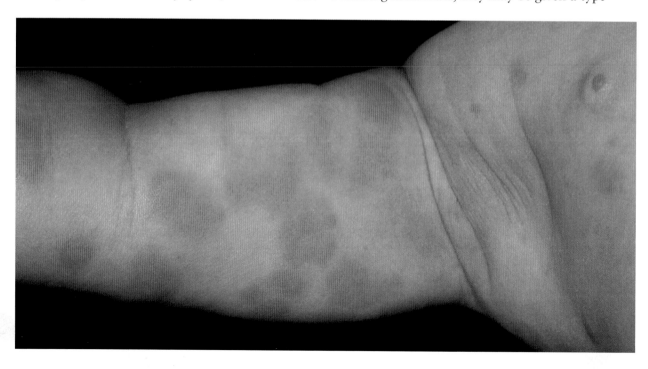

of inhaler. This contains a medicine that helps to reduce the swelling in the airways, making it easier to breathe normally.

Severe reactions

The only treatment for anaphylaxis, the most severe type of allergic reaction, is an injection of epinephrine (see page 21). A person suffering a severe reaction like this is treated as a medical emergency. They will probably be taken to hospital so that they can be monitored to make sure they recover completely.

▼ *This 10-year-old boy is in hospital undergoing a 'food challenge' to test for a food allergy. He will eat a variety of foods one by one, while being watched for symptoms of an allergic reaction by a doctor.*

ALICE'S DIAGNOSIS

Alice was 16 when she first experienced an allergic reaction. She had a scare when she suddenly found it very hard to breathe after eating a chocolate bar. She was suffering from anaphylaxis, and was taken to the Accident and Emergency department at the hospital by paramedics. Alice did not know why she was allergic to the chocolate. As she had such a severe reaction initially, they could not risk allowing her to come into contact with the allergen again, so some blood was taken to be tested.

Alice went back to the clinic after a few days to get the results of the tests. They showed that it was the peanuts in the chocolate bar that had caused her reaction.

A dietician explained to Alice that it was safe for her to eat chocolate again, but she would have to check the ingredients very carefully in the future, and she would also have to avoid coming into contact with peanuts in other foods and products.

Food allergies on the rise

Food allergies affect a lot of people. It has been estimated that as many as 15 million people in the USA suffer from a food allergy, around one person in every 27. In the UK, more than 1 million people have a food allergy.

Records show that food allergies have become more common in recent years – numbers have almost doubled during the last decade. There are several possible explanations for this, including:

Attitudes to food

In developed countries, the past 50 years or so have seen a gradual shift in the way we eat. Fresh, homemade meals make up a smaller proportion of a modern diet than in previous years. Instead, people now rely increasingly on processed foods and ready meals which have many different ingredients mixed in. It has also become more common to eat out in cafés and restaurants, and to grab quick meals at fast-food outlets.

▼ *Fast foods, such as hamburgers, often contain a variety of added chemicals. Research is also being carried out to discover whether different kinds of packaging play any part in food allergies.*

New foods

The increase in air transport has made it increasingly easy and cheap to obtain foods from anywhere in the world. This means we are now exposed to a much wider range of foods that we could possibly become allergic to. Scientists have also found ways to alter foods to create new types of food. Genetic engineers are now producing new food items, such as pluots (a cross between a plum and an apricot) and lematoes (a tomato that smells of lemon). This means that an allergen from one food could be transferred into a different food that we would not normally be allergic to.

Environment

In the past, people kept their homes clean by vacuuming and dusting, and kept themselves clean using soap. Today, we use many different types of chemicals in spray polishes and air fresheners, deodorants and other products. We are no longer exposed to as many substances, such as bacteria,

▲ *You are not likely to have seen any of these fruits in a shop! They are pluots, and have been created by genetically engineering plums and apricots.*

dust and dust mites, that used to be commonplace. Our immune systems may be weaker, or altered in other ways that mean they wrongly identify some foods as harmful.

Improved diagnosis

In the past, a person might be aware that when they ate a particular food they often felt ill. They would simply avoid the food and say that it 'didn't agree with them'. Now, scientific tests are available and food allergies are routinely diagnosed. This might mean that the proportion of people with food allergies has not really changed, but we are now better at diagnosing their conditions.

It seems likely that each of these factors plays some part in the apparent increase in the number of people in our society who suffer from food allergies.

Food allergies and families

People often notice how hair colour, eye colour or nose shape show how a child takes after his or her parents. The passing of characteristics from one generation to the next is called inheritance. Characteristics that are passed on in this way are said to be inherited. Is it possible that food allergies are inherited too? Or are allergies just brought about by the allergens that we are exposed to?

Inheriting allergies

Several studies have been made of families with a member who has a food allergy. Their findings suggest that food allergies are not inherited directly in the same way as characteristics such as eye colour. However, there does seem to be some genetic link between food allergies and other allergy problems such as hay fever, eczema and asthma.

Atopic families

Studies of many families indicate that what is inherited is not an allergy to a specific allergen, such as peanuts or milk. Instead, it is the tendency to develop an allergy that is passed on from parents to children. This tendency to develop allergies is called atopy, and families in which this is found are said to be atopic. The parents, brothers and sisters of a child with a food allergy are far more likely to have allergies themselves than the parents and siblings of a child without a food allergy.

GEOGRAPHY AND ALLERGIES

As well as genetic factors, environmental factors also play a part in the development of food allergies. For example, it has been found that a common allergy in one country will be different from a common allergy in another country, so allergies are linked to the general diet of the area. Thus, the most common allergy in Japanese children is soya allergy, while in New Zealand, children are more often allergic to eggs, and in Scandinavian countries, children are most often allergic to fish. Some food intolerances are also more common in some countries than in others. For example, many people of Chinese origin are unable to digest milk and dairy products. This is because the traditional Chinese diet does not include dairy products. Alcohol intolerance is also common in Asian people, with around one person in every two being affected.

In many atopic families, a wide range of different allergies is seen. Some family members may suffer from food allergies, such as peanut allergy or fish allergy. Some may suffer from allergies not related to food, such as hay fever and allergy to wasp stings or animal fur. Some may have both food and non-food related allergies.

▲ These girls look alike in many ways. They also look similar to their father. Like every one of us, they have inherited their features from their parents.

Genetics

The study of inheritance is called genetics. Inside every body cell are tiny chemical threads called chromosomes. Along the chromosomes, lined up like beads on a necklace, are tiny genes. It is these genes that control our characteristics, such as hair colour and nose shape. Some characteristics are controlled by a single gene. Others, including allergies, are more complicated, and are controlled by several or many genes. From studying atopic families, scientists think that the inheritance of atopy is probably controlled by a group of genes that lie close together on one chromosome. Research is still being carried out to identify the individual genes involved. It is hoped that, as scientists understand more about the inheritance of allergies, they may be able to develop improved ways of treating food allergies in the future.

Food allergies and age

Some food allergies begin at, or before, birth, some develop during childhood and others do not appear until adulthood. Some food allergies vanish as a child grows up, while others last throughout a person's life. These patterns are linked to the particular food a person is allergic to, and to the person's individual immune system.

▲ *A drink of milk at break time is a treat for many young children. Those with milk allergy, though, have to drink an alternative, such as water or fruit juice.*

Early childhood

Many children develop a food allergy during their first few years of life. The most common allergies found in early childhood are allergies to milk and egg. In recent years, peanut allergy has also become increasingly common in young children. Parents of very young children who have allergies need to monitor their diets carefully.

Childhood years

It is estimated that, by the age of five, 80 per cent of children with milk allergy or egg allergy will have outgrown them. Their immune system gradually stops reacting to the allergen. These allergies often seem to come and go together: a study in Australia found that 2 per cent of all children had milk allergy and 3.2 per cent had egg allergy – but more than half of the children with milk allergy also had egg allergy.

Not all children grow out of allergies, though. The more severe the allergy, the less likely it is to be outgrown. Also, children who have several different allergies are less likely to outgrow them than children with a single allergy. In a small proportion of children, milk and egg allergies persist throughout childhood and may last for life. Only about 20 per cent of children with peanut allergy will outgrow it. Allergies to other foods, such as tree nuts, may also start to develop during childhood. Parents still need to monitor their allergic child's food, but as they grow up, children become familiar with what they can and cannot eat.

▶ *As teenagers start to try new foods, there is a greater chance that they will develop an allergy to one of these foods.*

Teenage years

Teenagers often eat a more varied diet than they did when they were younger. This means that they may eat new foods, so new allergies may be diagnosed. Also, an allergy can develop to a food which could previously be eaten without causing any problem. Fish, shellfish, soya, peanut and wheat allergies may all arise during teenage years. As they become increasingly independent, teenagers are able to take full responsibility for managing their allergies.

Adulthood

Some allergies will persist from childhood throughout a person's life. New allergies, particularly to fish, shellfish, soya, peanut and wheat, can also arise. Adults who have food allergies need to monitor their diet just as closely as younger people with allergies.

Living with food allergies

Having a serious food allergy can affect many aspects of a person's life. He or she should wear a medic-alert bracelet and carry medicine at all times. Eating in restaurants, going to birthday parties and going on holiday are all things that need to be planned carefully in advance.

A person's food allergy can also affect their family and friends, and mean that special precautions have to be taken at school and other places they go to. However, as long as all the appropriate precautions are taken, having a food allergy should not stop someone doing just about anything they want to do.

Precautions at home

Having a family member with a serious food allergy means that the whole family must be aware of the allergy and be careful. Foods may have to be stored separately, and different meals prepared for the allergy sufferer. Some people are so allergic that just being in the same room as an allergen can trigger an allergic reaction, and so the rest of the family has to avoid having it in the house. Family members and friends can help a person with an allergy by being supportive and understanding, and by knowing what to do in an emergency.

For many young people with food allergies, it can be tough coping with the reaction from other people. They can find other people's attitudes quite unhelpful. Hopefully, as the general public becomes increasingly aware of food allergies, these problems will decline.

◀ *A girl on the beach, armed with an Epipen. Junior Epipens contain the exact quantity of epinephrine needed to treat a child's severe allergic reaction.*

▲ Peanuts used to be a common food served on airlines. However, many airlines now ban all peanuts and peanut products from their flights.

NADIA AND NUTS

Nadia, 16, has had a nut allergy since she was six years old.

'It's surprising, the number of things you have to check before you eat them. I always check the packets on chocolate bars, ready-made meals and ice creams, for example.

Even though I carry an Epipen with me all the time, I haven't had to use it yet. Once I felt ill at a party because of the traces of peanut dust that were in the air, but I managed to control my reaction with antihistamines.

Daily life is a lot easier than it used to be. Food labels are much clearer these days, showing whether they contain any traces of nuts. Travelling is easier too, now that peanuts are banned on many airlines, as well as schools and some colleges. Come to think of it, my food allergy really doesn't stop me from living the way I want to.'

Precautions at school

Most schools are happy to discuss a child's allergy with the family and to do their best to help. Every case is different and the needs of each child will be different, but typical steps include:

● discussing whether the child will be eating school lunches or taking a packed lunch

● making sure all staff are aware of the allergy and know what to do if a reaction begins

● making sure other pupils are aware of the allergy and understand why they must not share food with the allergic child

● making arrangements to keep the child's Epipen or other medication safe and quickly available for use

● ensuring the child does not come into contact with the allergen by accident – for example, through touching spilt milk.

21st century problems

Our eating patterns are changing and food allergies are on the increase. As we move further into the 21st century, how will food allergies change? Are we likely to see more kinds, or more frequent cases?

There seems to be no reason to hope that the current rise in the proportion of people with food allergies will stop or even slow down. Indeed, it might even increase, for several reasons:

Eating patterns

If we like a particular food, we tend to eat it often, thus increasing our exposure to any allergens it contains. As foods are now available all year round, our bodies do not have the natural break that used to occur as the seasons changed.

New allergens

GM foods are made by altering the genetic code of organisms. This may result in the creation of new allergens by the organism that would trigger new allergies in some people.

▼ *A handful of genetically modified soya beans.*

Mixing genes

Some GM foods are made by swapping a gene from one organism into another. It is possible that, for example, putting a peanut gene into a non-peanut organism could result in the food containing an allergen that would trigger a reaction in a person with peanut allergy. The person would not be aware of this, as the food label only has to show that it is a GM food, not give details of the exact way in which it has been modified. However, GM foods are tested to make sure that a food developed in this way does not trigger allergies.

Environment

As hygiene standards continue to be improved, our immune systems are exposed to fewer everyday allergens than in previous generations. It could be that our immune systems will weaken. This may result in the development of more food allergies.

New research

Despite all these factors which may contribute to increasing the number of food allergies, promising research is being carried out to improve the diagnosis and treatment of food allergies, to find vaccines and to produce allergen-free foods. Some scientists also believe a cure for food allergies will be found in the near future. It is hoped that, even if the proportion of people with food allergies does increase, scientific advances will make food allergies easier to live with.

▶ *The cleaning products we use are important and help us to avoid illnesses, such as food poisoning. However, some scientists think that this also means we are more likely to develop allergies.*

The future for food allergies

Scientists are following many lines of enquiry in the field of food allergies. There are research programmes attempting to understand more about allergic reactions, to improve diagnosis and treatments and to produce allergen-free foods.

There are many exciting breakthroughs in scientific research on food allergies. Here are some promising projects.

Interleukin-12

Scientists in Britain have discovered that the white blood cells of laboratory mice with a food allergy do not produce a chemical called interleukin-12. In normal mice, interleukin-12 keeps the immune system under control. Without it, the immune system can overreact. Other scientists are finding similar results in humans. It is hoped that injecting an allergen and interleukin-12 together may eventually be a possible cure for food allergies.

Altered allergens

Treatments for some allergies, such as hay fever, involve desensitising the person by injecting tiny doses of the allergen. This type of treatment is rarely used for food allergies, as the risks of a severe anaphylactic reaction are too high.

▶ *Interleukin-12 has a complicated structure with spirals and straight parts. It plays an important part in controlling the immune system. Scientists hope it may help them to develop new ways of treating food allergies.*

However, scientists in the Netherlands have identified the chemical allergen responsible for allergy to apple. They then created a very similar chemical in a laboratory. IgE antibodies do not bind to the laboratory allergen and so an allergic response does not occur. Scientists in the US are carrying out similar work with peanut allergen. Early results suggest that injections of tiny doses of the new chemicals may provide a safe way to desensitise the immune systems of people with food allergies.

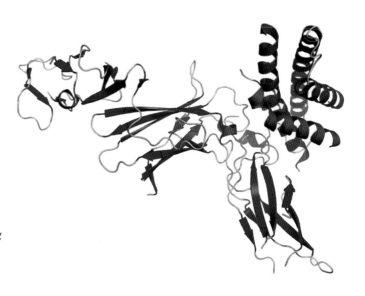

Allergen-free foods

Scientists worldwide are also trying to develop allergen-free foods. There are several different approaches to this, including:

Destroying allergens

Some foods containing allergens can be treated to destroy the allergen they contain. The food can then safely be eaten by a person who would normally be allergic to it. An example of this is 'Fine Rice', which has been developed in Japan. Normal rice contains globulin, a protein to which some people are allergic. By treating rice with chemicals to destroy the globulin, a safe product, Fine Rice, is produced.

Genetic engineering

The same process that may create new allergens can also help to develop allergen-free foods. There are two stages. First, the scientists identify the precise chemical structure of an allergen. Then they alter the genetic code of the food crop to make it produce a slightly different chemical that does not trigger an allergic reaction. The race is on to develop a GM peanut which does not contain the three proteins that trigger the most allergic reactions. Research groups all around the world are working on developing it. However, the problem is that by taking enough of the allergens out of a peanut, the GM peanut will simply not taste like a peanut any more. It may be many years before an allergy-free GM peanut can be produced.

Radiation treatment

This can result in changes in the genetic code of an organism. These changes can give rise to new organisms with characteristics that differ from the

▲ *The rice seedlings in these dishes are the result of genetic engineering. This technique can produce allergen-free crops.*

original organism. Scientists using this technique in Japan have developed an allergen-free soya bean.

Although serious food allergies can be difficult to live with, things should get easier in the future, thanks to better labelling, new tests and treatments, and greater awareness among the general public.

Glossary

adrenaline another name for epinephrine

allergen a chemical that triggers an allergic reaction

allergic reaction a response by the immune system to an allergen

allergist a doctor who specialises in the diagnosis and treatment of allergies

allergy a sensitivity or a reaction to something that is harmless to most people

anaphylaxis a severe type of allergic reaction

antihistamine a medicine that combats the effects of histamine

asthma a condition that causes breathing difficulties

atopy inherited tendency to develop allergies

characteristic a feature of something or someone

circulation the movement of blood through the veins of the body

cross-contamination when chemicals in one substance come into contact with, and mix with, another substance

dietician a person who specialises in planning diets and giving advice about them

eczema a type of skin rash

enzyme a chemical that controls the speed of a chemical reaction in the body

epinephrine a hormone that the body produces when under stress. Made in a laboratory, it is a chemical used to treat anaphylaxis

Epipen a syringe filled with one dose of epinephrine, used in case of anaphylaxis

food aversion extreme dislike of a particular food

food intolerance inability to digest a particular food

gelatin a transparent, brittle protein

gene the basic unit of heredity by which characteristics are passed from one generation to the next

genetic influenced by genes inherited from parents

gluten a substance found in cereals, such as oats and wheat

GM (genetic modification) changing the genetic code of an organism

hay fever an allergic reaction to pollen that can make your nose, throat and eyes itch and your nose run

histamine a substance that is released by the body when it is injured or invaded by germs or other external particles

IgE antibody a chemical made in response to a first exposure to an allergen

immune system mechanisms that protect the body from germs and diseases

inheritance the process of passing on physical characteristics from parents to their offspring

lactase an enzyme that breaks down lactose

lactose a type of sugar found in milk and milk products

lymphocyte a type of white blood cell that can produce IgE antibodies

mast cell a type of white blood cell that releases histamine

outpatient session a visit to a doctor by a patient which does not involve staying overnight in a hospital or clinic

particles very small pieces

protein a type of complex biological chemical. Proteins are the material that is used to make blood cells, body tissue, hormones and other important substances

psychological to do with the mind

symptoms changes in the body that can indicate that a disease or other condition is present

tofu a cheese-like food made from soya milk

tree nuts nuts such as walnuts, hazelnuts, cashews, pecans and almonds

vaccine substance given to improve immunity to a specific disease

white blood cells cells in the blood that kill germs

Further information

Books

Fiction

Peter Can't Eat Peanuts, Nadine O'Reilly, *O'Reilly Publishing Inc, March 2006*

The Peanut Butter Jam, Elizabeth Sussman Nassau, *Health Press (NM), June 2001*

Non-Fiction

Allergy Information for Teens: Health Tips about Allergic Reactions Such as Anaphylaxis, Respiratory Problems, and Rashes (Teen Health), Karen Bellenir, *Omnigraphics; 1 edition, January 2006*

Peanut Butter, Milk, and Other Deadly Threats: What You Should Know about Food Allergies (Issues in Focus Today), Sherri Mabry Gordon, *Enslow Publishers, June 2006*

Special Diets and Food Allergies (Making Healthy Food Choices), Carol Ballard, *Heinemann, January 2007*

The Peanut Allergy Answer Book: 2nd Edition, Michael C Young, *Fair Winds Press, August 2006*

I'm Hungry: Easy Family Recipes Free From Milk, Egg, Soya, Wheat, Gluten, Tanya Wright, *DoctorZed Publishing, August 2012*

Websites

www.allergy.org.au
ASCIA (Australasian Society of Clinical Immunology and Allergy)
The Ascia website offers information about what a food allergy is, statistics about the most common food allergies and the latest news and research.

www.allergyfacts.org.au
Anaphylaxis Australia promotes awareness of the dangers of anaphylaxis with educational schemes, research and support. Read the story about John and Jane and watch a cartoon on the Kid's Corner page of their website.

www.allergyinschools.org.uk
The 'Allergy in Schools' website, run by the Anaphylaxis Campaign, has tips for students and teachers for making sure that snacks and lunches in schools are safe for people with food allergies. The 'Students' page explains what allergies are, what to do in an emergency and how schools can help support the Anaphylaxis Campaign.

www.allergyuk.org
Allergy UK is a medical charity established to represent the views and needs of people with allergy, food intolerance and chemical sensitivity. The website publishes food alerts and a helpline number for those who think they might be allergic to certain foods.

www.foodallergy.org

Food Allergy Initiative is a US organisation offering up-to-date news and advice on living with food allergies and how to cater for people with food allergies.

www.kidswithfoodallergies.org

The Kids With Food Allergies website offers recipes, information and discussion forums for parents and families of children with allergies.

www.kidshealth.org/kid/ill_injure/sick/ food_allergies.html

The Kidshealth website is part of the Nemours Mission. It provides information about food allergies, with opportunity to ask questions and receive feedback. Other areas of the website provide information about all aspects of teenage health and well-being.

Note to parents and teachers: Every effort has been made by the Publishers to ensure that these websites are suitable for children, that they are of the highest educational value, and that they contain no inappropriate or offensive material. However, because of the nature of the Internet, it is impossible to guarantee that the contents of these sites will not be altered. We strongly advise that Internet access is supervised by a responsible adult.

Index

These are the list of contents for each title
in Explaining:

Asthma

What is asthma? • History of asthma • Increase in asthma • Who has asthma? • Healthy lungs • How asthma affects the lungs • What triggers asthma? • Asthma and allergies • Diagnosing asthma • Preventing an attack • Relieving an attack • What to do during an attack • Growing up with asthma • Living with asthma • Asthma and exercise • Future

Autism

What is autism? • Autism: a brief history • The rise of autism • The autistic spectrum • The signs of autism • Autism and inheritance • The triggers of autism • Autism and the body • Autism and mental health • Can autism be treated? • Living with autism • Autism and families • Autism and school • Asperger syndrome • Autism and adulthood • The future for autism

Blindness

What is blindness? • Causes and effects • Visual impairment • Colour blindness and night blindness • Eye tests • Treatments and cures • Coping with blindness • Optical aids • Guide dogs and canes • Home life • On the move • Blindness and families • Blindness at school • Blindness as an adult • Blindness, sport and leisure • The future for blindness

Cerebral Palsy

What is cerebral palsy? • The causes of cerebral palsy • Diagnosis • Types of cerebral palsy • Other effects of cerebral palsy • Managing cerebral palsy • Other support • Technological support • Communication • How it feels • Everyday life • Being at school • Cerebral palsy and the family • Into adulthood • Raising awareness • The future

Cystic Fibrosis

What is cystic fibrosis? • A brief history • What causes cystic fibrosis? • Screening and diagnosis • The effects of cystic fibrosis • How is cystic fibrosis managed? • Infections and illness • A special diet • Clearing the airways • Physical exercise • Cystic fibrosis and families • Cystic fibrosis at school • Living with cystic fibrosis • Living longer • New treatments • Gene therapy

Deafness

What is deafness? • Ears and sounds • Types of deafness • Causes of deafness • Signs of deafness • Diagnosis • Treating deafness • Lip reading • Sign language • Deafness and education • Schools for the deaf • Deafness and adulthood • Technology • Deafness and the family • Fighting discrimination • Latest research

Diabetes

What is diabetes? • Type 1 diabetes • Type 2 diabetes • Symptoms and diagnosis • Medication • Hypoglycaemia • Eyes, skin and feet • Other health issues • Healthy eating and drinking • Physical activity • Living with diabetes • Diabetes and families • Diabetes at school • Growing up with diabetes • The future for diabetics

Down's syndrome

What is Down's syndrome? • Changing attitudes • Who has Down's Syndrome? • What are chromosomes? • The extra chromosome • Individual differences • Health problems • Testing for Down's Syndrome • Diagnosing at birth • Babies • Toddlers • At school • Friendships and fun • Effects on the family • Living independently • Down's syndrome community

Epilepsy

What is epilepsy? • Causes and effects • Who has epilepsy? • Partial seizures • Generalised seizures • Triggers • Diagnosis • How you can help • Controlling epilepsy • Taking medicines • Living with epilepsy • Epilepsy and families • Epilepsy at school • Sport and leisure • Growing up with epilepsy • The future for epilepsy

Food allergy

What are food allergies? • Food allergies: a brief history • Food aversion, intolerance or allergy? • What is an allergic reaction? • Food allergies: common culprits • Anaphylaxis • Testing for food allergies • Avoiding allergic reactions • Treating allergic reactions • Food allergies on the rise • Food allergies and families • Food allergies and age • Living with food allergies • 21st century problems • The future for food allergies